Dare to Dream and Soar Like an Eagle —

The Sky's the Limit!

Success Principles That Will Transform Your Life

Published by
Miranda Burnette Ministries

Cover Design by Jackie Moore

Printed in the United States.

ISBN 13: 978-0692276242

ISBN 10: 0692276246

For more information or to order books contact:

Miranda Burnette Ministries

Email
miranda@mirnadaburnetteministries.org

Website
www.mirandaburnetteministries.org

Dedication

I dedicate this book to my t h r e e beautiful grandchildren, Shanice, Shannon, and LaTrelle Jr. They are the joy of my heart. I love them very much! As they grow older, I want them to *Dare to Dream and Soar Like an Eagle*—to go from level to level in all they do, realizing that they can do all things through Christ, Who strengthens them.

> *I have strength for all things in Christ, Who empowers me.*
> *[I am ready for anything and equal to anything through*
> *Him Who infuses inner strength into me; I am self-*
> *sufficient in Christ's sufficiency.]*
> *—Philippians 4:13*

Table of Contents

Foreword

Dare to Dream and Soar Like an Eagle will help you create a shift in your mindset, develop a larger vision for your life, and start dreaming big dreams. It will also challenge you to expand your possibilities!

So many times we become satisfied and stagnant. At those times, we need something or someone to help us dream and expand the vision for the possibilities that are ahead. We often look at the problems rather than the possibilities, the obstacles rather than the opportunities. Once we expand our vision, we expand our possibilities.

The information in this book is delivered in an easy-to-understand format, but it will make a powerful impact on your life because of its basic success strategies and principles. As you read them, your mind will be fed and you will begin to grow to another level.

This is not a book you should read just once. Read it over and over again so that the words and principles will become a part of your subconscious programming. It is what you read and hear consistently that will be manifested in your life. If you want to change your life, you must change your mindset. This can begin by reading and applying the information in this book. Take time to experience the powerful principles and thoughts that Miranda Burnette has put together. Dare to dream the big dreams and soar like an eagle, because the sky is the limit.

Mike Howard
Peak Performance Speaker
Author of *From Ordinary to
EXTRAordinary: Success Begins Within*

Introduction

Do you have goals, dreams, ideals or visions of things you want to do, be or have in your life? I think everyone has a dream deep down on the inside!

> *If there were dreams to sell, what would you buy?*
> —*Thomas Lowell Beddoes*

Your dream may be to have your own business, pay off your home, earn a higher degree, or make lots of money. Young people may have a dream of becoming a doctor, lawyer or great athlete. Your goal may be to just get out of debt or graduate from college!

What's your dream? When I use the word *dream*, I'm not referring to the type of dream most of us have while sleeping. That dream is a series of thoughts, mental images or emotions occurring during sleep. I am also not referring to a daydream, which is a dream-like fantasy experienced while awake.

The type of dream I'm talking about is a condition or achievement that is longed for, an aspiration, a cherished desire, an idea, a vision, a goal, an aim.

I dare you to go after your dreams. Have you ever been dared to do something? I'm sure you have, even if it was when you were a child.

Children are always daring one another to do something. When someone dares you to do something, it is usually not an easy thing to do, and there is often a risk involved. That sometimes makes us want to do it even more to prove to the darer that we are capable of handling the task.

So I dare you and encourage you to take the challenge set out in this book: Dare to be great and soar like an eagle—the sky's the limit!

Unless stated otherwise, all Bible scriptures are from the New International Version, the Amplified Version or the King James Version.

Chapter 1
Dare to Dream

> *A dream is the bearer of a new possibility, the enlarged horizon, the great hope.*
> *—Howard Thurman*

Each of us has a dream in our hearts. It's the thing we were born to do. Our dreams are related to our purpose in life. A dream provides an outlet for our greatness to be released and increases our potential!

With a dream, we begin to see ourselves in a new light, as having greater potential and being capable of stretching and growing to reach it.

Every resource we discover, every talent we develop, and every opportunity we meet becomes a part of our potential to grow toward that dream. The greater the dream, the greater the potential. If your dream is great, so is your potential for success!

A dream provides us with something worthwhile to aim for. Until we have identified the right direction, we will never know for sure that our movement is actually progress. Our actions are just as likely to take us backward instead of forward.

A dream helps us prioritize. People with dreams are willing to give up certain things in order to go to the next level. They measure everything they do according to whether or not it contributes to their dream. They concentrate their attention on the things that bring them closer to their dreams, and give less attention to everything that doesn't!

A dream solves problems for others. It puts everything we do in perspective and provides us with purpose to help us serve and meet the needs of others.

Dreams help us to be other-focused. Even the tasks that are not exciting or immediately rewarding take on added value when we know they ultimately contribute to helping others. We are called to help increase the kingdom of God.

Dare to dream and act on those dreams in spite of circumstances, problems or obstacles. You can pursue your dream no matter where you are today. What happened in the past isn't as important as what lies ahead!

> *We grow great by dreams. All big men are dreamers. They see things in the soft haze of a spring day or in the red fire of a long winter's evening. Some of us let these dreams die, but others nourish and protect them, nurse them through bad days till they bring them to the sunshine and light that comes always to those who hope that their dreams will come true.*
> *—Woodrow Wilson*

Dare To Dream

*Let nothing hold you back from
exploring your wildest fantasies,
wishes and aspirations.
Don't be afraid to dream big
and to follow your dreams
wherever they may lead you.
Open your eyes to their beauty;
open your mind to their magic;
open your heart to their possibilities.*

*Dare to dream.
Whether they are in color
or in black and white,
whether they are big or small,
easily attainable or almost impossible,
look to your dreams,
and make them become reality.
Wishes and hopes are nothing
until you take the first step
toward making them something!*

*Dare to dream,
because only by dreaming
will you ever discover
who you are, what you want,
and what you can do.
Don't be afraid to take risks,
to become involved,
to make a commitment.
Do whatever it takes to make
your dreams come true.
Always believe in miracles,
and always believe in you!*

—Julie Anne Ford, from Cybernation.com

Dreams and Visions are Possible

Dreams and visions for our future are possibilities, but not "positive-lies." This means that all things are possible, but they are not positively going to happen. We have to cooperate with God and do our part.

> *For the dream comes through much effort and the voice of a fool through many words.*
> *—Ecclesiastes 5:3 (NASB)*

The plan and vision that God has for your life may be difficult at times, but it is always worth the effort. Don't give up when times get tough, and remember to never despise the day of small beginnings. You have to do something. You have to put forth effort. Dreams don't work unless you do.

> *I dream of big things. I work for the small things. If you're going to dream, you might as well dream big. A lot of that came from my mother. She was adamant about the work ethic— about how you can't just dream things.*
> *—Kevin Costner*

> *How do you go from where you are to where you want to be? I think you have to have an enthusiasm for life. You have to have a dream—a goal—and you have to be willing to work for it.*
> *—Jim Valvano*

If you are determined to put in the effort, you will see God perform miracles in your life. The dreams and visions He gives us for our future are possibilities, but it takes our cooperation, willingness, determination, obedience and hard work to develop what He has put in us.

> *Knowing is not enough; we must apply.*
> *Willing is not enough; we must do.*
> —*Johann Wolfgang von Goethe*

If you are not dreaming, you are cheating yourself. If you don't have a dream, a goal and a purpose in life, you're never going to become whom God intended you to be. A person who refuses to give up will always succeed eventually!

> *The work goes on, the cause endures, the hope still lives,*
> *and the dreams shall never die.*
> —*Edward Kennedy*

> *Now to Him Who, by [in consequence of] the [action of*
> *His] power that is at work within us, is able to [carry out*
> *His purpose and] do superabundantly, far over and above*
> *all that we dare ask or think [infinitely beyond our highest*
> *prayers, desires, thoughts, hopes or dreams].*
> —*Ephesians 3:20*

The biggest way we limit God is through our unwillingness to acknowledge His bigness in our dreaming!

God told me to:

Think big!

Dream big!

Plan big!

Expect big things!

He is saying the same thing to you today!

If you don't expect much, you won't get much, so raise your level of expectation. God does not give you a dream without also giving you a plan to make the dream a reality.

Daring Dreams

Daring dreams inspire you to work hard because you know that one day your dream will become a reality. They motivate you to pay the price to achieve them. Everything worth having costs something. The better the desired results, the higher the price. In other words, excellence costs more than average. You don't have to put forth the effort for *average* that you have to put forth for *excellence.*

Daring dreams motivate you to take smart risks to achieve your dream, to step out on faith, to make a change.

Daring dreams build you up and encourage you. They make you feel like you can accomplish something great. They motivate you to keep going when times get tough. They help you press on when people talk about you or put you down.

Daring dreams will benefit others around you. It's not all about you. When it comes to success, it is about achieving goals and visions and improving yourself so you will be better equipped to help others achieve their goals.

Dare to Dream and Soar Like an Eagle

> *A goal is a dream with a deadline.*
> *—Napoleon Hill*

Daring dreams rely on discipline. We have to be disciplined to be successful. Daring dreams lead to action. We can't just *dream* we have to do something; we must *do* something. We are deceiving ourselves if we think we can dream and not do something to work toward those dreams.

> *So also faith, if it does not have works*
> *[deeds and actions of obedience to back it up],*
> *by itself is destitute of power [inoperative, dead].*
> *—James 2:17*

James 1:22 says to be doers of the Word [obey the message], and not merely listeners to it, betraying yourselves into deception by reasoning contrary to the Truth.

Daring dreams make you responsible and give you accountability. They give you the ability to make and keep commitments. Many people don't realize the responsibility of the upward journey. Taking total responsibility for your life is one of the most important things you can ever do! Accepting complete responsibility for all your actions represents maturity in your life.

When you accept complete responsibility, success and achievement will follow. Once you accept total responsibility for every decision you make and every action you take, there is nothing you can't do, have and accomplish.

9

> *I believe that every right implies a responsibility;*
> *every opportunity, an obligation;*
> *every possession a duty.*
> *—John D. Rockefeller, Jr.*

> *Happy are those who dream dreams and are ready to pay*
> *the price to make them come true.*
> *—Cardinal Leon J. Suenens*

Too many people are ready to assert their rights, but not to assume the duties and responsibilities that go with those rights.

> *So those [who now] are last will be first [then],*
> *and those who are first will be last.*
> *For many are called, but few chosen.*
> *—Matthew 20:16*

> *But he who did not know and did things worthy of a beat-*
> *ing shall be beaten with few [lashes]. For everyone to*
> *whom much is given, of him shall much be required; and of*
> *him to whom men entrust much, they will require and de-*
> *mand all the more.*
> *—Luke 12:48*

Daring dreams, and accepting the responsibility for them, have changed the world. Industry pioneer and visionary Henry Ford had a daring dream. He built his first car in a shed behind his house. He continued to think about how to improve his early efforts, and he studied the work of other car builders. Out of his passion for machinery, and his intrigue over the automobile, grew Ford's dream: the creation of an inexpensive mass-produced automobile. In 1903, he organized Ford Motor Company and began to produce the Model T. He has been credited with the birth of the assembly line and mass production. Ford's dream became a reality.

John F. Kennedy had a daring dream too: to put a man on the moon.

Martin Luther King Jr. had a daring dream—a dream of equality. As the old saying goes, what the mind can conceive and believe, it can achieve!

> *Every great dream begins with a dreamer. Always remember, you have within you the strength, the patience, and the passion to reach for the stars to change the world.*
> *—Harriet Tubman*

Dream Development Stages
The seed stage. The seed may be a vision that grows out of the desire in your heart. God puts desires in our hearts. In fact, sometimes He will lead us with desire. God might reveal your dream to you in a time of prayer, or you may be motivated by an event from your everyday life. (See Chapter 3.)

The commitment stage. Once you discover your dream, go after it! Les Brown, a renowned motivational speaker, puts it this way: "Find out what you want and go after it as if your life depends on it. Why? Because it does."

> *Whatever your hand finds to do,*
> *do it with all your might.*
> *—Ecclesiastes 9:10*

It will take determination, commitment, hunger and tenacity to see a dream through until it becomes a reality.

The development stage. When dreams are new, they are fragile because they haven't had time to grow and develop. They are not established yet. For example, when a seedling oak is only a year old, a child can tear it out by the roots, but once it has had some time to become firmly established, even the force of a hurricane can't knock it down.

Dreams are also more easily torn down at this stage. If dreams are quickly attacked, it is usually done by close friends or family members, since they are the only ones who know about them. Our dreams and ideas may be able to weather the criticism of a stranger, but they have a difficult time surviving when criticized by a loved one! Don't allow their words to stop you. Don't let anyone steal your dream!

It's also possible that you are hindering yourself. God has spoken, or tried to speak, some great things to some of you, and you have said, "That is impossible, that could never happen." Perhaps it is impossible for people alone, but with God all things are possible.

The living-it stage. If you are dedicated and determined, and you persevere, you will reach the living-it stage of your dream. You may have to survive the doubts and criticisms of people closest to you, but you can make it to the living-it stage. Some people just don't realize how close they are to living their dreams.

> *Keep your dreams alive. Understand [that] to achieve any-thing requires faith and belief in yourself, vision, hard work, determination and dedication. Remember all things are possible for those who believe.*
> —*Gail Devers*

The supporters stage. People of vision need the support of those around them. (Everyone will not want to celebrate with you when your dream begins to become a reality.) There are several characteristics of supporters: they are encouragers and willing helpers, cooperative and dependable, and have a winning attitude.

Sometimes, when you are trying to realize your dreams, you will be surprised by which people want to support you and which ones do not want to, and will not, support you. Some people you consider friends will reject you and fight against your success. There will also be people who will support you in ways you didn't expect. They will help your dream to become a reality.

No matter who undermines you, criticizes you or puts you down, don't let them stop you. Keep your focus on your dream and keep pressing on.

The sharing stage. A big part of what it means to be successful is sharing your dreams with others. People react in one of two ways when they realize their dream: Some people hold their dream close and try to keep all of it for themselves. But when they hold the dream close, it usually gets smaller. Because they don't get the help of others, they don't experience the joy of sharing their blessings with others. People who share their dream will have the privilege of seeing it grow.

The helping stage. Once your dream is realized, you should help others live their dreams. It's not all about us. God wants to touch others' lives through us. As He blesses us, He wants us to be a blessing to others. But the manifestation of our God-given dreams does not appear overnight. It grows from a seed planted in our heart by God and nourished and nurtured by us day after day until it gradually springs forth as fruit in our lives. (See Chapter 3.)

> *The mightiest works have been accomplished by men who have kept their ability to dream great dreams.*
> *—Walter Bowie*

> *So many of our dreams at first seem impossible, then they seem improbable, and then, when we summon the will, they soon become inevitable.*
> —Christopher Reeve

> *Build a dream and the dream will build you.*
> —Robert Schuller

Chapter 2
Clarify Your Vision

A dream (a cherished desire) gives you hope for a better tomorrow—something to look forward to. A vision (the formation of a mental image of something that is not perceived as real and is not present yet) gives us direction. You can't fulfill your purpose and grow toward your potential if you don't know what direction you should be going!

> *You see things and you say, "Why?"*
> *But I dream things that never were*
> *and I say, "Why not?"*
> —*George Bernard Shaw*

Vision is something we see in our minds—a mental focus of the way things could, or should, be in the near future. It involves the way we think about our past, our future and ourselves.

What do you see in your future? What do you see yourself accomplishing? What is your vision?

Vision is not about what is happening right now; that doesn't matter. Just because things are not going well doesn't mean they will be that way forever. You should see yourself coming out of, or being out of, the situation. You should begin to speak about yourself and your situation in a positive way. Then your actions will follow and you will begin to form the right habits that will lead to good character. The good character goes on to lead to your destiny. And it will all start with a mental sight of your vision.

Vision is very powerful. It allows you to look past your circumstances, see your God-given potential, and open the door for God to do the impossible through your life! It enables you to believe that God will provide bigger and greater things. Faith moves God to help us.

> *And Jesus said, ["You have asked Me],*
> *'If You [Jesus] can do anything'?*
> *[Why], all things can be [are possible]*
> *to him who believes!"*
> *—Mark 9:23*

> *They can conquer who believe they can.*
> *—Virgil*

Vision may be something God plants in us or something we see on purpose. It might be a calling God has for our lives, something He wants us to do. Or it could be a desire for something we want to see happen in our lives, so we see it on purpose.

In order to fulfill your dreams, your vision must be secure. You have to believe in yourself and have a positive self-image. You can't let what others say about you, or the way they treat you, determine your self-worth. You have to believe that you are worthy of what you desire and see yourself as an achiever, an overcomer, or a capable person.

> *If you can control a man's thinking, you don't have to worry about his actions. If you can determine what a man thinks, you do not have to worry about what he will do. If you can make a man believe that he is inferior, you don't have to compel him to seek an inferior status; he will do so without being told. And if you can make a man believe that he is justly an outcast, you don't have to order him to the back door; he will go to the back door on his own and, if there is no back door, the very nature of the man will demand that you build one.*
> *—Carter G. Woodson*

A vision is a deeply burning desire that motivates people to venture into new territories without allowing shortcomings to paralyze their progress. A vision focuses on the future.

> *Where there is no vision [no redemptive revelation of God], the people perish; but he who keeps the law [of God, which includes that of man], blessed [happy, fortunate and enviable] is he.*
> *—Proverbs 29:18*

Unless you have some visions, goals or dreams, you perish in your spirit. You lose your enthusiasm! You lose your get-up-and-go! You are not motivated! People without a vision usually become passive, inactive or lazy. They also get bored, and often become negative, critical and judgmental of others who *are* pursuing their dreams.

People of vision are focused on a goal. People without vision lack the passion and desire to keep moving forward. The consequences of not having vision are often a lack of true spiritual fulfillment. Helen Keller said, "To have sight without vision would be worse than being born blind."

Take a look around you and notice the tall buildings, schools, houses, highways, machines, airplanes, ships and so forth. Everything you see that is manmade was first a vision in somebody's mind. All things start as visions, which become big dreams. Then, when that dream is implemented, it becomes a reality. All great accomplishers have been motivated by their dreams!

> *Do not [earnestly] remember the former things; neither consider the things of old. Behold I am doing a new thing! Now it springs forth; do you not perceive and know it and will you not give heed to it? I will even make a way in the wilderness and rivers in the desert.*
> *—Isaiah 43:18-19*

People of vision have *purpose* (an object toward which they strive; an aim; a goal, direction, dream, plan, reason or mission) and *passion*:

Passion
Passion is a strong or extravagant fondness, enthusiasm or desire for something. It's also referred to as affection, dedication, devotion, fondness, craving, aspiration, admiration or energy.

When it comes to what makes people successful, passion for their vision makes the difference. Passion is fuel for your will. When you have passion, you do something because you love it and you give it everything you've got! Passion is what makes it possible for people who might seem ordinary to achieve great things!

> *What happens when you believe something with all your heart? Belief fuels enthusiasm, and determined enthusiasm explodes into passion.*
> *—Mac Anderson*

> *Nothing great was ever achieved*
> *without enthusiasm.*
> *—Ralph Waldo Emerson*

You must be passionate—excited—about your dreams and visions. If you're not excited about your own dreams, how can you expect other people to be charged up about them and support them?

Passion motivates you to do your best, and to go above and beyond what is expected. It helps you go the extra mile, motivates you to do what you have to do to get that higher degree or that promotion. Passion will give you the strength to stay up all night to study if you have to. It will help you achieve your fondest goal.

My vision, driven by my passion, motivated me when I was working on my degrees at Troy State University. I had to drive two hours there and two hours back at night after working all day. When I think about that situation, I wonder how I did it. I was often so tired on the way back from class that I had to pull off the road to rest at a gas station. I realize now that my passion motivated me. The Lord put the desire in my heart to earn those degrees and He gave me the vision and passion I needed to achieve them. He also gave me the strength to drive up and down the dangerous highways, and He protected me.

Passion will motivate you to work hard and give your dream the time needed to make it a reality. Passion changes you! It will help you step out of your comfort zone, inspire you to do what it takes to reach the top, help you to overcome your fears to reach your goals, enable you to do things that are out of the ordinary for you, and help you have the patience and endurance that it takes to develop your potential.

Passion increases your willpower and creates such a desire in your heart for something that you will be willing to make great sacrifices to accomplish it. Nothing can be substituted for passion! You can't help but become a more dedicated, productive person if you follow your passion toward your vision.

Press On

Sometimes we just have to press on (exert steady force or pressure). Almost nothing worthwhile happens in our lives without pressing. Paul said he "strained" forward—he was determined, and he said that was the most important thing to him. Fulfilling your destiny demands letting go of what lies behind. The vision of the future has no place for the failures of the past.

> *If we take care of the inches,*
> *we will not have to worry about the miles.*
> *—Hartley Coleridge*

> *I do not consider, brethren, that I have captured and made it my own [yet]; but one thing I do [it is my one aspirations], forgetting what lies behind and straining forward to what lies ahead, I press toward the goal to win the prize to which God in Christ Jesus is*
> *calling us upward.*
> *—Philippians 3:13-14*

> *And no one pours new wine into old wineskins; if he does, the fresh wine will burst the skins and it will be spilled and the skins will be ruined [destroyed].*
> *—Luke 5:37*

Wine is made by putting grapes through a press. You have to press those grapes to get the juice that eventually becomes wine. Just like oil, wine often represents the power of the Holy Spirit in our lives. Power can't be given to someone who is hanging on to old ways.

When Jesus says, "You can't pour new wine into old wineskins," He is basically saying that you can't put new power into somebody who is not ready for it, not prepared, or holding on to old things and old ways. If you mix old and new, both can be ruined!

How do we get that power? We have to press! Pressing makes us stronger. When you press weights, it's hard, and sometimes it hurts, but the result is that you are stronger and more fit, and you are prepared for whatever task you have to do. You are a better person physically because you pressed through.

You will also be a better person spiritually if you press, and more prepared for whatever God has for you to do. Only people who press turn out to do great works for God and make their visions a reality. We have to press out of the past into the future!

When we are pursuing our dreams, we have to press through many things, such as hard times, trials, criticism, the desire to give up, depression and discouragement. The past is like a magnet; it keeps trying to draw us back. We have to resist the pull. The woman who had been bleeding for 18 years, who had spent all she had on doctors and was no better, pressed through the crowd to touch Jesus.

> *And a certain woman, which had an issue of blood for twelve years, and had suffered many things of many physicians, and had spent all that she had, and was nothing bettered, but rather grew worse. When she had heard of Jesus, came in the press behind, and touched His garment.*
> —Mark 5:25-27

> *Nothing in this world can take the place of persistence.*
> *Talent will not; nothing is more common than unsuccessful*
> *people with talent. Genius will not; unrewarded genius is*
> *almost a proverb. Education will not; the world is full of*
> *educated derelicts. Persistence and determination alone are*
> *omnipotent. The slogan "press on" has solved, and always*
> *will solve, the problems of the human race.*
> *—Calvin Coolidge*

You have to let go of what lies behind and press forward. If you don't, the past will destroy your future. Look straight ahead; don't look back. If runners in a race keep looking back, it will slow them down; we don't want anything to slow us down. We want to make progress. So forget the past, shake it off, bury it.

> *I like the dreams of the future better*
> *than the history of the past.*
> *—Thomas Jefferson*

Vision also stretches reality beyond its current boundaries. Some people may tell you that what you're doing is impossible, but that shouldn't make you give up. The Bible tells us that all things are possible with God. Even a vision for ministry is given by God because it conveys His purpose and points to the direction He wants the ministry to follow.

> *Jesus glanced around at them and said,*
> *"With men, [it is] impossible, but not with*
> *God, for all things are possible with God."*
> *—Mark 10:27*

Hope

Hope is favorable and confident expectations, the happy anticipation of good. Hope put off or delayed leads to disappointment. God wants to give you the desires of your heart!

> *Hope deferred makes the heart sick, but when the desire is fulfilled, it is a tree of life.*
> *—Proverbs 13:12*

> *Now faith is the assurance [confirmation, the title deed] of the things [we] hope for, being the proof of things [we] do not see and the conviction of their reality [faith perceiving as real fact what is not revealed to the senses].*
> *—Hebrews 11:1*

People who have a vision given by God have hope based on faith. They are certain of what they hope for but do not yet see. People with a vision think big and dream big! They test their dreams and ideas with God's Word and know that God's vision is usually larger than their abilities, because it takes God's power and resources to carry out His plans!

If you wait until everything is just right, you will never step out to make your dreams a reality! You will never soar like the eagle!

> *He who observes the wind [and waits for all conditions to be favorable] will not sow [do good], and he who regards the clouds will not reap [get back good].*
> *—Ecclesiastes 11:4*

If we magnify every little difficulty, or start projects and continue to imagine hardships and trouble when there are none, we will never go on with our work! People with a vision are willing to pay the price to achieve their visionary product. They know that it is the implementation of a vision that sets men and women apart from their peers.

> *And my God will liberally supply [fill to the full]*
> *your every need according to His riches in glory in*
> *Christ Jesus.*
> *—Philippians 4:19*

People of vision are people of honor, integrity and excellence. (Excellence doesn't mean *perfect*, it means doing your best.) People with a vision do not use other people to meet their needs.

People of vision ask for help when they need it, but they also willingly share their success with those who help them. They believe in service, they help others succeed, they don't give up too soon, and they aim high. They invest in the goals God has given them!

Goals

> *It must be borne in mind that the tragedy of life does not lie*
> *in not reaching your goals; the tragedy lies in not having*
> *any goals to reach. It isn't a calamity to die with dreams*
> *unfulfilled, but it is a calamity not to dream. It is not a dis-*
> *aster to be unable to capture your ideals, but*
> *it is a disaster to have no ideas to capture. It is not a*
> *disgrace not to reach the stars, but it is a disgrace*
> *to have no stars to reach.*
> *—Dr. Benjamin Isaiah Mays*

Continue to dream big dreams, but also realize that the short-term goals that take you to the next levels of your vision are the real keys to success.

The Value of Vision

The following list contains examples of how a strong God-given vision motivated some of the worthwhile accomplishments recorded in the Bible.

Leader	Vision
Abraham (Genesis 12)	To create a great nation of people of faith
Moses (Exodus 3, 4)	To lead the people of Israel out of Egypt
Joshua (Numbers 27)	To lead the people of Israel into the Promised Land
David (1 Chronicles 22)	To build the temple in Jerusalem
Solomon (2 Chronicles 28)	To complete the building of the temple
Nehemiah (Nehemiah 2)	To rebuild the Jerusalem wall
Esther (Esther 4)	To save the Jewish people from Haman
Zerubbabel (Haggai 1)	To rebuild the temple
Jesus (Matthew 28; Luke 15)	To seek and save the lost, and to disciple men to do the same
Paul (Acts 9)	To take the gospel to the Jews and Gentiles

Miranda Burnette

Write Your Vision

> *And the Lord answered me and said, "Write the vision and engrave it so plainly upon tables that everyone who passes may [be able to] read [it easily and quickly] as he hastens by.*
>
> *For the vision is yet for an appointed time and it hastens to the end [fulfillment]; it will not deceive or disappoint. Though it tarries, wait [earnestly] for it, because it will surely come; it will not be behind on its appointed day.*
> *—Habakkuk 2: 2, 3*

Vision is using your imagination (the ability to form mental images of things or events) to visualize the goal God has given you for your life, the plan He has laid out for you.

> *Ask and it will be given to you; seek and you will find; knock and the door will be opened to you. For everyone who asks receives; he who seeks finds; and to him who knocks, the door will be opened.*
> *—Matthew 7:7-8*

Many times God unfolds His plan as we start to move in a direction and trust Him to lead. What we need to do is seek God's plans for our lives and then write down what we believe God is saying to us.

Through Habakkuk, God furnishes some instructions on vision for all of us. A divine vision:

Should be written down (v. 2).

Should be distributed to people (v. 2).

Should be acted on (v. 2).

Is for a select time in the future (v. 3).

Motivates us toward the goal (v. 3).

Should not be discarded (v. 3).

Will not fail (v. 3).

God will do what He said He is going to do!

In hope of eternal life, which God, [Who] cannot lie, promised before the world began.
—Titus 1:2

That by two immutable things, in which it was impossible for God to lie, we might have a strong consolation, who have fled for refuge to lay hold upon the hope set before us.
—Hebrews 6:18

Focus

As we began to move in a certain direction, what we are supposed to do with our lives will become increasingly clear. Make sure you don't lose sight of your vision. Keep it in front of you. Stay focused!

Also, if we try to do too many things, we won't be effective in any of them! We can't major in minor things and have the success we desire.

> *If you chase two rabbits, both will escape.*
> *—Unknown*

Have you ever wondered why experienced animal trainers take a stool when they step into a cage with a lion? When the trainer holds the stool with the legs extended toward the lion's face, the lion tries to focus on all four legs at once. And that paralyzes him.

In the same way, when *we* try to focus on too many things at once, it paralyzes us. We get stuck and we don't make any progress because we are not giving any of those things the time and attention that is needed to make them successful. We can't do everything!

Divided focus always works against you. You have to keep your eyes on the prize and be single-minded toward your vision!

In order to stay focused, you may need to heed the advice of Habakkuk: Write your vision and make it plain. Habakkuk 2:3 speaks of an "appointed time" for a vision to come to pass. "Appointed time" means that God knows when the time is right. We might not know, but He does.

We may move too fast or too slow. We may say, "Let's wait," but God may say, "Step out now, move now." We may say, "Let's step out and make the move now," but God may say, "Wait." We must humble ourselves and our ideas to God's wisdom and power, and we must trust Him when He says He will not be late.

"Appointed time" also means a time already established by God and decided for certain reasons. An example is when we have an appointment with a doctor. We can't have access to the doctor until our appointment time has come. We can't go earlier and, if we are late, we will still not be able to see the doctor. If we go at the appointed time, we get treated quickly.

In the same way, God has "appointments" for specific things in our lives that will happen at their scheduled times. They will not be early, and they will not be late. They will happen for us at God's appointed time.

It is vitally important for each of us to have a vision for our lives. Let's begin to dream and, while we are dreaming, let's dream big, because we serve a big God Who loves us and wants the best for us!

> *So shall you find favor, good understanding and high es-*
> *teem in the sight [or judgment] of God and man.*
> *—Proverbs 3:4*

> *Yet amid all these things we are more than conquerors and*
> *gain a surpassing victory through Him*
> *Who loved us.*
> *—Romans 8:37*

> *Whatever you can do or dream you can, begin it.*
> *Boldness has genius, power, and magic in it.*
> *—Johann Wolfgang von Goethe*

> *To accomplish great things, we must dream as well as act.*
> *—Anatole France*

> *But thanks be to God, Who in Christ always leads us in triumph [as trophies of Christ's victory] and through us spreads and makes evident the fragrance of the knowledge of God everywhere.*
> *—Corinthians 2:14*

Chapter 3
Plant Seeds of Greatness

Think about a peach seed. In its natural form, it's just a seed. But, if it is planted under the right conditions at the right time and taken care of properly, it will grow into a beautiful, flourishing, fruit-bearing peach tree. Everything starts with a seed because thoughts are seeds!

> *Another story by way of comparison He set forth before them, saying, "The kingdom of heaven is like a grain of mustard seed, which a man took and sowed in his field.*
>
> *"Of all the seeds, it is the smallest, but when it has grown, it is the largest of the garden herbs and becomes a tree, so that the birds of the air come and find shelter in its branches."*
> *—Matthew 13:31-32*

> *While the earth remains, seedtime and harvest, cold and heat, summer and winter, and day and night shall not cease.*
> *—Genesis 8:22*

What we think eventually comes out in some form or fashion: attitudes, moods, words, actions.

> *Do not be deceived and deluded and misled. God will not allow Himself to be sneered at [scorned, disdained, or mocked by mere pretensions or professions, or by His precepts begin set aside]. [He inevitably deludes himself who attempts to delude God.] For whatever a man sows, that, and that only, is what he will reap.*
> *—Galatians 6:7*

Thoughts determine the outcome of our lives!

> *As he [a man] thinketh in his heart, so is he.*
> or
> *As a man thinks in his heart, so does he become.*
> *—Proverbs 23:7*

> *You are never too old to set another goal or to dream a new dream.*
> *—C. S. Lewis*

> *Watch your thoughts, they become words.*
> *Watch your words, they become actions.*
> *Watch your actions, they become habits.*
> *Watch your habits, they become character.*
> *Watch your character, it becomes your destiny!*
> *—Frank Outlaw*

Words are seeds that produce a harvest based on the type of seeds they are—positive or negative. Each word we speak is like placing a seed in the ground. If you sow positive words, you will have a positive life. If you sow negative words, you will have a negative life. What you sow is what you are going to get. Just as sure as they are planted, you can be equally sure a harvest will follow!

Cultivate Inspired Ideas

Ideas are also like seeds! They must be saved, cultivated (improved in excellence or condition), watered, pruned and developed, or they will not bear fruit. Everything starts with a seed! God wants to give each of us inspired ideas, and one inspired idea can change your entire life!

When you get an idea, you need to ask yourself: "Is my idea based on my own feelings, or is it God's idea according to His plan of success for my life?"

> *Roll your works upon the Lord. [Commit and trust them*
> *wholly to Him. He will cause your thoughts to become*
> *agreeable to His will, and] so shall your plans be*
> *established and succeed.*
> *—Proverbs 16:3*

This means that you must trust God with every area of your life, your family, your marriage, your health, your work—everything.

You need to choose to give God's Word first place in your decisions. If you do, He will cause your thoughts to become agreeable to His will. Then your plans will be established and will succeed!

> *Lean on, trust in, and be confident in the Lord with all your heart and mind, and do not rely on your own insight or understanding. In all your ways, know, recognize and acknowledge Him, and He will direct and make straight and plain your paths.*
> *—Proverbs 3:5, 6*

God will give you creative, inspired ideas (guided, controlled, communicated or suggested by divine influence) and, if you act on them according to His plan, they will successfully come to pass.

Inspired ideas come in different forms:

1. A hunch: An idea or belief based on feelings or suspicions rather than on clear evidence (walking by faith); a guess, belief, suspicion, or opinion. You have a gut feeling or you sense something.

2. A strong thought that won't go away. For example, you might say to yourself, "I think I'll start my own business." You really have a desire to do it, but then you say, "I don't have the education" or "I don't have time." Then you go about your business, but the thought keeps coming back to you—it just won't go away.

3. Intuition: A keen and quick insight about something.

4. A "knowing": Something you know deep inside. You don't know why, but you just know. You think to yourself, "I just know I am supposed to be a teacher. I just know it." You just know that you know that you know. It's like a revelation from God.

Your ideas and your vision will give you the dreams you need to soar like an eagle. If only you will dare!

God's Word Is also a Seed

*And when a very great throng was gathering together and
people from town after town kept coming to Jesus, He said
in a parable:*

*"A sower went out to sow seed and, as he sowed, some fell
along the traveled path and were trodden underfoot, and
the birds of the air ate it up. And some [seed] fell on the
rock and, as soon as it sprouted, it withered away because it
had no moisture. And other [seed] fell in the midst of the
thorns, and the thorns grew up with it and choked it.
"[And] some seed fell into good soil, and grew up and
yielded a crop a hundred times [as great]."*

*As He said these things, He called out, "He who has ears to
hear, let him be listening and let him consider and understand by hearing."*

*And when His disciples asked Him the meaning of this
parable, He said to them, "To you it has been given [has
come progressively] to know [recognize and understand
more strongly and clearly] the mysteries and
secrets of the kingdom of God, but for others, they are in
parables, so that [through] looking, they may not see; and
hearing, they may not comprehend.*

*"Now the meaning of this parable is this:
The seed is the Word of God."
—Luke 8:4-11*

You and I started out as a seed in the wombs of our mothers. We didn't appear immediately—there is a nine-month development period. We can't have a harvest without seedtime!

> *Victory is won not in miles but in inches.*
> *Win a little now, hold your ground,*
> *and later, win a little more.*
> *—Louis L'Amour*

> *Inch by inch, life's a cinch.*
> *Yard by yard, it's really hard.*
> *—Morgan Wootten*

Unfortunately, seedtime usually means giving up something that is valuable to you now in order to have something later on that you consider to be more precious!

> *I assure you, most solemnly I tell you. Unless a grain of wheat falls into the earth and dies, it remains [never becomes more, but it lives] by itself alone. But if it dies, it produces many others and yields a rich harvest.*
> *—John 12:24*

That little seed can feel like the gardener (God) is punishing it and being mean to it. But really He is only helping it to become what it was intended to be in the first place.

Sometimes we also feel like God is punishing *us* when we go through different trials, but again, it's so He can make us into the person that He wants us to be.

Be assured and understand that the trial and proving of your faith bring out endurance and steadfastness and patience.

But let endurance and steadfastness and patience have full play and do a thorough work, so that you may be [people] perfectly and fully developed [with no defects], lacking in nothing.
—James 1: 3-4

If God had intended for a peach seed to stay a seed, He would not have put a peach inside. If God had intended for you to stay as you are, He would not have put the seed of an idea, a dream, a vision or greatness inside you! The key to achieving greatness is found when we discover and then develop our dreams. It is all inside of you, just waiting to be released!

God starts with a seed, which He plants in us in the form of a thought, dream or desire. In order for that seed to grow and develop, we must nourish and nurture it, being careful to watch over it and protect it. The Devil is a dream thief. He will use decent well-meaning people to try to discourage you—people who don't even know He is using them. So don't listen to critical people. The bigger your dream, the more people you will be able to help!

God uses the pattern of birthing in many areas of our lives. First, in order to become pregnant, you need to *believe* that the vision God has placed in your heart is possible. It is during this stage that a dream is a *possibility* but not a *positively*. Again, this means that all things are possible, but they are not positively going to happen.

In your life, you have to conceive (become pregnant with, form in your mind, think or imagine) that your dream is possible. What can you conceive in your mind? We have to conceive it on the inside before we are ever going to receive it on the outside!

If we nourish and protect our seed, one day it will spring forth as the manifestation we desire. But we have to be careful, because the Devil will use all kinds of tactics to steal the seed of our dreams.

> *The thief [Devil] comes only in order to steal and kill and destroy. I came that they may have and enjoy life, and have it in abundance [to the full, until it overflows].*
> —*John 10:10*

Once physical conception has occurred, there is much planning and preparation before the actual birth. During the spiritual preparation stage, you need to be aware that Satan will attempt to get you to "birth" prematurely. You may go through various phases and feel things you have never felt before. You may be frightened, tired of waiting, or simply not understand what's going on.

Finally it's time for delivery! That may sound exciting, but actually it is the hardest part of all. Hold on to your dreams and vision and give birth to all that God has placed in your heart!

All of God's creations (including you) have in their possession the hidden ability to be greater than they are right now! In you at this very moment are the seeds to be all God created you to be! Only God can take you from where you are to the life He has destined you to live. So let the seeds of greatness God has placed in you be unleashed!

Dig Deep

There is a goldmine of dreams, visions, abilities and strengths hidden in every life, but you have to dig to get it. You must be willing to go beyond how you feel now or what is convenient. If you dig down deep into your spirit, you will do greater things than anyone could ever imagine. That is why there is so much power in an inspired idea!

> *The secret of success is to do the common*
> *things uncommonly well.*
> —*John D. Rockefeller, Jr.*

What Rockefeller is saying is that everyone has the possibility of greatness or success. Many times we have wonderfully inspired ideas, but we don't act on them. Then we miss the very thing God is trying to accomplish for us.

God wants us to be big thinkers! You can't be a little thinker and expect God to give you big ideas. If the idea is inspired by God, He will show you what steps to take so you can soar like an eagle!

> *Beloved, I pray that you may prosper in every way and*
> *[that your body] may keep well, even as [I know] your soul*
> *keeps well and prospers.*
> —*3 John 2*

> *For God so greatly loved and dearly prized the world*
> *that He [even] gave up His only begotten Son, so that*
> *whosoever believes in [trusts in, clings to, relies on]*
> *Him shall not perish [come to destruction, be lost] but*
> *have eternal [everlasting] life.*
> —*John 3:16*

> *The key to realizing a dream is to focus not on success but significance—and then even the small steps and little victories along your path will take on greater meaning.*
> *—Oprah Winfrey*

> *The future belongs to those who believe in the beauty of their dreams.*
> *—Eleanor Roosevelt*

Chapter 4
Recognize that God Created You for Success

God has a plan for your life, and He is ready to help you achieve it. Success is within your grasp if you are willing to take the first step and pursue the dream He has given you. He's not with-holding your success from you until you're perfect. He wants you to pursue it today.

> *What is not started today is*
> *never finished tomorrow.*
> *—Johann Wolfgang von Goethe*

We see this truth in the life of Joseph, son of Jacob. Joseph dreamed big dreams, and what was his brothers' response? They said, "Look, the dreamer is coming; let's kill him now."

> *And they said one to another, "See, here comes this dreamer and master of dreams. So come on now, let us kill him and throw his body into some pit; then we will say [to our father], some wild and ferocious animal has devoured him; and we shall see what will become of his dreams!*
> —Genesis 37:19-20

Joseph was a man with a dream from God, yet he wasn't a perfect person. He was young and, in some ways, immature when God spoke to him. But his age and immaturity didn't keep God from reaching out to him.

The story of Joseph also reminds us to be persistent. In pursuing his dream, he faced many challenges: His brothers didn't appreciate his dream and sold him into slavery. He was falsely accused and wrongly imprisoned. He was forsaken and forgotten by many people.

Yet everywhere Joseph went, he rose to the top, and his dream not only prospered him, but it saved his entire family from famine. Why? Because he had a dream from God and he wouldn't let go of it. It took 13 years before Joseph's dream began to bear fruit.

Your dream won't manifest overnight either but, when it comes to pass, it will be a far greater blessing than you can imagine. So, no matter what happens, you must commit to pursuing your dream.

Encourage yourself with scriptures, such as Philippians 4:13: "I can do all things through Christ Who strengthens me."

God is our designer. He knows our innate capabilities better than anyone. Like all good designers, He provided us with a manual—the Bible—to help us on the journey of developing our potential. When we apply God's Word to our lives, we discover that we can be so much more than we are right now. Building our lives on the solid foundation of the Word promises to bring great success!

> *Do not let this book of the law depart from your mouth.*
> *Meditate on it day and night so that you may be careful to*
> *do everything written in it. Then you will be*
> *prosperous and successful.*
> *—Joshua 1:8*

Meditation on the Word of God is vitally important, because it is the key to success in every area of our lives. The Word has inherent power in it. The phrase in Joshua 1:8, "Meditate on it day and night" means to ponder it, dwell on it, take it and turn it over and over in your mind.

Why? So you can do everything written in it. As we meditate on the Word of God, power is released to help us to do as the Bible says—it enables us to live what God commands.

Successful and Unsuccessful People

> *The difference between a successful person and others is*
> *not a lack of strength, not a lack of knowledge, but*
> *rather a lack of will.*
> *—Vince Lombardi*

Successful people are motivated by a vision beyond themselves, bigger than themselves! They have something that constantly keeps them going. It is out of their reach, and yet they believe that if they work hard enough, they will someday hold that dream in their hands!

Successful people reject rejection. People who achieve their dreams don't give up trying, because they don't base their self-worth on their performance. You must understand that what you do is not who you are—you are who the Word of God says you are. You can do what God says you can do, and you can have what the Word of God says you can have!

Our value is in our identity (who we are in Christ), not in our performance. You may not do everything right, but God looks to your heart. We should find value in who we are in Christ, not what we do! Just because you failed at something doesn't mean that you are a failure. Success is a process.

Walt Disney was fired from a newspaper because he lacked ideas. Later he went bankrupt several times before he built Disneyland. NBA superstar Michael Jordon was once cut from his high school basketball team. Henry Ford failed and went broke five times before he succeeded. Best-selling author Max Lucado had his first book rejected by 14 publishers before finding one that was willing to give him a chance. That describes a successful person!

Unsuccessful people are only motivated by today; they are not tomorrow-thinkers. They don't look beyond themselves. They grab the present with eagerness, not even taking into consideration what tomorrow may bring to them. You should have a vision for a future that is not determined by your past or your present circumstances so you can soar as high as an eagle!

Chapter 5
Have a Good Plan

People of vision have unbending confidence in the almighty God. They don't wait for success to be handed to them—they go for it! They develop a plan to implement their dream. They put their time, effort and finances into it. They are focused on their dreams.

Take a positive look at the possibilities God has planned for you.

> *"For I know the thoughts and plans that I have for you,"* says the Lord, *"thoughts and plans for welfare and peace and not for evil, to give you hope in your final outcome."*
> —*Jeremiah 29:11*

God has a perfect plan for your life—a plan of success. But we have to participate in that plan for it to come true. We have to cooperate with God as He prepares us for the plan He has for our lives—for the things He wants to give us at different stages in our spiritual growth—when we are spiritually and physically ready. If we gave our children things they were not adult enough to handle, we wouldn't be very good parents; we could be putting them in danger.

Just like a natural parent, God will not give us something, even prosperity or success, that we are not spiritually mature enough to handle, because it might bring danger to us. And He loves us just like we love our own children. He will give us only what we are able to handle, but He wants to bless us above and beyond. Are you prepared for what God has prepared for you?

> For we are God's [own] handiwork [His workmanship], recreated in Christ Jesus [born anew], that we may do those good works which God predestined [planned beforehand] for us [taking paths which He prepared ahead of time] that we should walk in them [living the good life which He prearranged and make ready for us to live].
> —Ephesians 2:10

God has prepared a good life for us, but we must be ready to receive it. He had a good plan for us before we were even born, and He wants us to have an abundant life.

> Beloved, I pray that you may prosper in every way and [that your body] may keep well, even as [I know] your soul keeps well and prospers.
> —3 John 2

> *But on the contrary, as the scripture says, what eye has not seen and ear has not heard and has not entered into the heart of man [all that] God has prepared [made and keeps ready] for those who love Him [who hold Him in affectionate reverence, promptly obeying Him and gratefully recognizing the benefits He has bestowed].*
> *—1 Corinthians 2:9*

When you discover what you were made for, your heart rejoices! Pastor Creflo Dollar teaches us that, when you find your destiny, you will also find your prosperity!

> *As it is written, I have made you [Abraham] the father of many nations. [He was appointed our father] in the sight of God in Whom [he] believed, Who gives life to the dead and speaks of the nonexistent things that [He has foretold and promised as if they [already] existed.*
> *—Romans 4:17*

Begin to call those things that aren't yet as though they were. Think and speak about your future in a positive way. Prophesy your future. Speak your future into existence!

All realistic visions can be achieved if they are well planned, managed and cultivated by people filled with faith in God and willing to pay the price it takes to soar!

Miranda Burnette

> *Even if you are on the right track, you'll get*
> *run over if you just sit there.*
> *—Will Rogers*

> *And the Lord shall make you the head, and not the tail,*
> *and you shall be above only, and you shall not be beneath,*
> *if you heed the commandments of the Lord your God,*
> *which I command you this day, and are watchful*
> *to do them.*
> *—Deuteronomy 28:13*

Chapter 6
Soar Like an Eagle

In the Bible, the eagle is used as a simile (connects two unlike things by drawing like comparisons).

> *But they that wait upon the Lord shall renew their strength; they shall mount up with wings as eagles; they shall run and not be weary; and they shall walk and not faint.*
> *—Isaiah 40:31*

God created the eagle in such a way that it would be an example to us. He chose this bird to motivate us to reach our full potential in life.

Eagles are majestic, magnificent, powerful and full of dignity. They are considered king of the birds. They are the symbol of a conqueror, and they have a great sense of purpose. Eagles dwell on rocks in the high places of the earth. They are committed, they are reliable mates, and they are devoted parents. Christian eagles are also bold, strong and fiercely devoted.

The eagle is confident enough to stand alone in life against the storms, to spread its wings and soar above the clouds of destruction. Always remember this: Birds fly in flocks, but eagles fly alone.

If you want to be an eagle for God, and do what He has called you to do, you must learn how to stand alone. It doesn't matter whether everybody is cheering you on or not!

Other birds are content to live inside the boundaries that others set for them, but eagles can never be satisfied with such a limited life— they must be free!

> *You cannot fly like an eagle with wings of a wren.*
> *—William James*

The Word of God says, in John 8:36: "So if the Son liberates you [makes you free men], then you are really and unquestionably free."

Other birds are afraid of everything, but eagles are afraid of nothing. The eagle only reaches its full potential by how it handles the adversity that comes. Adversity and trials also help us to grow and be strong—they bring us into our full potential.

> *For God hath not given us the spirit of fear; but of power,*
> *and of love, and of a sound mind.*
> *—2 Timothy 1:7*

The eagle can sense a storm even before it sees one, but it never runs for cover or tries to get away from it. The eagle uses the storm to lift it to higher places!

> *The way of the eagle is too wonderful to understand.*
> *—Proverbs 30:18-19*

> *There are three things which are too wonderful for me, yes, four which I do not understand:*
>
> *The way of an eagle in the air, the way of a serpent upon a rock, the way of a ship in the midst of the sea, and the way of a man with a maid.*
> *—Proverbs 30:18-19*

> *No bird soars too high if he soars with his own wings.*
> *—William Blake*

Commitment

Commitment is the key to victorious living; it is the way of the eagle. Commitment is inherent (built in). It is part of the eagle's behavior. The eagle is a remarkable, majestic bird that has tremendous strength in its wings, which can span up to seven feet. The eagle does not flap, it soars!

> *Unless commitment is made, there are only promises and hopes ... no plans.*
> *—Peter Drucker*

> *Does the eagle mount up at your command and make*
> *his nest on [a] high [inaccessible place]?*
>
> *On the cliff he dwells and remains securely,*
> *upon the point of the rock and the stronghold.*
>
> *From there he spies out the prey;*
> *and his eyes see it afar off.*
> *—Job 39:27-29*

Eagles have the best eyesight of any bird. They can see a rabbit from two miles in the air, and see two miles in any direction.

Eagles also have focus; they allow nothing to distract them. They will struggle and persevere against all odds. The eagle is born a tenacious fighter. It never gives up or quits; and once it takes hold of a prey, it will die rather than give it up.

Eagle Story

An eagle was kept as a pet for 10 years, confined to the limitations of life in a cage. One day his owner decided to set him free. The sky was his true territory. There would be no limits there; he would be living where he was really created to live!

It was a cloudy day when the eagle was placed outside his cage, and he just stood there. Would he fly? Would he be unable to fly? He hadn't flown for 10 years, and he wasn't familiar with the real world outside of his cage.

As the eagle stood there looking around, the clouds parted and the sun came out. A ray of sunlight hit right where he was standing and, when he saw the light, it was as if it sparked new life in him.

He opened up his wings ... he flapped them in place for a moment ... and suddenly he was flying. He was free!

He had somehow received the power to function in a new world—a world he had never known before. He had dared to begin a new life!

Some of you have also been living a limited life—a life without meaning and power. Maybe it was caused by circumstances such as past failures, bad relationships, negative people or low self-esteem. Maybe it was caused by the ongoing negative words of others. Some of you may not even understand that there is a whole new world for you to enter.

Some people have been in situations for so long that they think that is the way things are supposed to be. They may say, "That is just the way it is." They don't even try to get out of a bad situation and go after their dreams.

We were born to win, but many have been conditioned to lose. If we can be conditioned to lose, we can also be conditioned to win and succeed. It's time for the "light" to hit you too. I'm not talking about the sunlight that hit the eagle. God's Word is light!

> *Your word is a lamp to my feet and a light to my path.*
> *—Psalm 119:105*

God is saying to you today, "Dare to begin your new life." The Word of God will lead you, guide you, and strengthen you. It will help you fly like an eagle and go to higher heights—from level to higher levels in the Lord. The sky's the limit. It's time for you to stretch your wings and soar!

Miranda Burnette

Miranda Burnette is the president and founder of Miranda Burnette Ministries, Inc. She is also a licensed evangelist. She travels and holds Success Seminars that teach people how to discover and fulfill their calling, to make their dreams a reality, to be successful in every area of their lives, and to be all that God intended for them to be. The vision of Miranda Burnette Ministries is to educate, equip and empower others to be successful leaders and reach their full potential.

Miranda is the author of *Success Starts in Your Mind, A Manual on How to Think Your Way to Success.* She is the publisher of *Keys to Success* magazine. *Keys to Success* magazine is a monthly magazine received by the friends and partners of Miranda Burnette Ministries. Miranda hosts a weekly Radio Program, *Keys to Successful Living.* She also makes an impact on the lives of others with her teachings on DVD and CD.

She is the founder and president of I Can Christian Academy, Inc.

Miranda and her husband, Morris lives in Atlanta, Georgia and are the parents of two adult children, LaTrelle and Davin.

www.ingramcontent.com/pod-product-compliance
Lightning Source LLC
Chambersburg PA
CBHW060050050426
42448CB00011B/2376